# A MONTH
# VOLPAIA, TUSCANY

## *Diary of a "Temporary Citizen"*

*"I thank you for the wonderful words
you wrote on Volpaia."*

Giovannella Stianti Mascheroni, Castello di Volpaia

*"The place and characters are deeply enchanting.
It is reminiscent of wonderful ethnographic pieces I've read.
The photos are terrific!"*

Doria Reagan, Psychologist

*"With deep feeling for his adopted home-away-from-home,
Bob has produced a charming evocation of this little-
known spot… just the thing for Italophiles wishing to stray
from the tourist-beaten track or who long to travel in a way
that involves being as well as seeing."*

Ron Reagan, Radio/Television Political Commentator and Author

*"I have spent many days in Italy, many near the vine.
Life has never cheated me or mine. Yet reading Robert's
notes and signs, I sense I've yet to grasp what was there
all this time. A luscious blooming rosemary, a sweet scented
fig, an aria echoing from ancient stone halls, a café with no
walls. Temporary citizenship acknowledges
time and place without need for more from this or
any distant shore. It's life, enjoy it!"*

Tom Douglas, Author and Restaurateur

# A MONTH IN MEDIEVAL VOLPAIA, TUSCANY

## *Diary of a "Temporary Citizen"*

BY
ROBERT P. CROSBY
WITH
PATRICIA N. CROSBY

Vivo! Publishing Co., Inc.

Vivo! Publishing Co., Inc.
1916 Pike Place, Suite 12
Box 1303
Seattle, Washington 98101

Designed by Gayle Goldman
Cover photo: copyright of Claudio Beduschi - www.beduschi.com


ISBN: 978-09776900-2-2

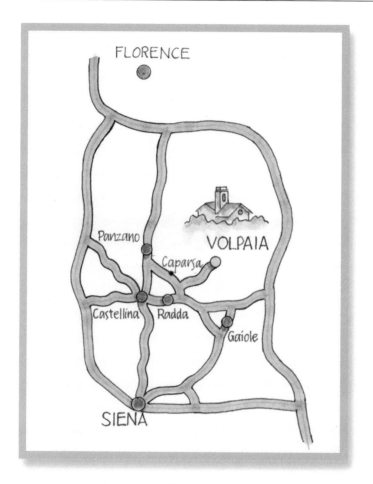

DEDICATED TO:

The Barucci family, *Volpaia*

Kim and Dario Cecchini, *Panzano*

The Cianferoni family, *Caparsa Vineyards*

# ACKNOWLEDGEMENTS

Elizabeth Smith entered my handwritten diary into her computer and then patiently, laboriously, and voluntarily continued through various edits. Many thanks!

Jack van Kinsbergen gifted me with Photoshop work that several commercial shops said they couldn't do.

Kyle D. T. Reynolds of Pike & Western Wine shop graciously offered research and editing help. He helped locate restaurants in Italy and translated e-mails into Italian for me. Kyle has both U.S. and Italian citizenship.

Gioia Milani, answered numerous email inquiries and was exceptionally responsive and helpful in adding accuracy to details in this story.

Gayle Goldman, as in previous books of mine across 16 years, gave her special touch as a graphic designer, layout artist, and constant consultant about many facets of this project.

Tina Morelli of La Scuola Italiana, my teacher, carefully edited giving special attention to her native Italian language. Grammar, both English and Italian, improved significantly after her touch.

Dr. Donald Williamson, a pre-eminent family therapist and friend provided insights into the human condition and alerted me to possibilities at various places in the text where deeper meaning could be explored.

Steve Pappas, an artist and a friend who is a doorman at our condo in Seattle, created the map featuring Volpaia, by far the smallest of all the towns on this map, Caparsa, the farm and winery of the Cianferoni family, Panzano, the home of Dario and Kim Cecchini, and other towns mentioned in my story. Thank you Stavros, as I call him.

Thanks to readers Jean and Lloyd Brelsford, George Shinn, Patricia Smith, and Doria Reagan for helpful comments.

# ABOUT THE AUTHORS

Robert P. Crosby has been a lifelong educator beginning with a two-decade career in outdoor education emphasizing the interdependence of all life.

In 1969 he founded the LIOS Institute where Patricia also taught for 15 years in the graduate program. LIOS is now thriving as the LIOS Graduate College of Saybrook University. He has authored a number of books and articles.

While the diary is Robert's, Patricia's influence permeates the story and includes excerpts written by her while in Volpaia.

His formal degrees are from Otterbein University, United Theological Seminary (Dayton, Ohio,) and Boston University. Bastyr granted him an L.H.D.

Her formal degrees are from Eastern Washington University and City University (Seattle) through the Masters Program at LIOS.

# TABLE OF CONTENTS

# ON BEING A "TEMPORARY CITIZEN"

This is my story of a recent month in a medieval Tuscan town of 52 year- round residents. Patricia and I discovered and "fell in love" with the people and ambiance of Volpaia about a decade ago. We now spend a month each year in "temporary" residence in a rental 300 feet from the piazza (town square) pictured and described in what follows.

Originally, I was writing this diary for my own record. I was not writing as a sociologist or historian about Volpaia (though that would be a worthy task) but about my experience there as a "temporary citizen". Soon, my purpose became more expansive. I want to invite your imagination to join us in this experience. I do hope that my genuine appreciation, affection, and yes, love for others comes through in the midst of my writing about their warm-hearted response to me. With editing, the diary has become more like a memoir.

Acknowledging the acclaim of others directed toward me and then accepting that deep within has been a life journey for me – as I know it has been for others. These experiences in Volpaia have been very satisfying and I have not edited out the acclaim coming my way. I believe I have brushed up against that deep part of humanity in myself that is loved simply because I exist. As Thomas Merton, the Trappist Monk has so beautifully written, "It is the unaccepted self that stands in my way and will continue to do so as long as it is not accepted"[1].

I carry with me an unending curiosity about others – their life stories, beliefs, and a need to embrace and be embraced by ethnic groups different from my own. To be a "temporary citizen", a phrase I first heard from Rick Steves, the travel guru, I believe one needs such a curiosity plus a deep respect for their culture, religious expression, history, and language. I studied Italian intensely this last year and with recordings over the past twelve years. I still know little and yet enough to converse as I note in this diary. Most of my conversations are with older villagers who speak only Italian.

---

1. Merton, T., A Year with Thomas Merton: Harper San Francisco, 2004 (Entry for October 10)

A way in which I join is in song. I'm an amateur tenor, but good enough to sing solos frequently and have sung with many male quartets and choirs across my 82 years. For twenty years, I sang with the late Jim Hinde at Seattle's Pike Market. In a front page obituary, a Seattle newspaper called him, "….the soul of the Market". I often join the rhythmic and harmonious African American group, "A Moment in Time" [2], for a couple of songs. Also, I know the lyrics to many Italian opera arias, Neapolitan folk songs, and Latin sacred music. The choice to learn Italian music and join the culture in this way has opened many doors to these spirited, music-loving people. Upon reading this, a friend commented:

> "In this book you highlight the capacity for life long pursuit done purely as an 'amateur' (for the the love of it!) – in your case singing, which is your great gift (the passion and the voice.) I imagine that in Volpaia all the singers are amateur. They love to sing and to listen whenever the occasion arises. And they value what you have to share – song. Spontaneous eruption is pretty rare in the U.S. No?" [3]

What is the magic of this experience? Most readers of our first draft responded, "I want to go there!"

But the magic lies, not in going, seeing, or doing. The elixir is being! The primary ingredient of the magic is the capacity to be present with the other(s). Not there to be a photographer or to collect souvenirs, though these can also be fun, but as a human with humans. To experience the abundant life one needs to create the magic of "presence", one with the other.

Salute!

---

2. Levi, Kenny, Johnie, James, Everett, and Cliff
3. Patricia Smith, Seattle

# About Volpaia

Volpaia is a village recorded as early as the 12th century. It is known for the remnants of a castle, Castello di Volpaia, which was built in the 12th and 13th centuries and for its deserved reputation as a medieval gem. It lies midway between Florence and Siena, near Radda in Chianti, and became a main fortress for Florence in the jurisdiction called the Chianti League. It retains a great deal of it's original architecture which has been carefully maintained and restored by the Stianti Mascheroni family since the 1970's. Some restorations now provide exquisite lodgings for tourists. One of these, Frantoio, is a stage for this diary. The ancient local greenish-grey sandstone provides a background for the lavish flora of the area. The population in 1427 was 117 persons. In 1833 it had 256. Today, 52.

The castle shop sells high quality Chianti Classico, Vin Santo, Balifico – a sangiovese and cabernet sauvignon blend, plus other wines from the Volpaia winery owned by the Stianti family. Their olive oil and vinegar are among other items offered. All wines are highly rated. Some have received the coveted Three Glasses rating. Volpaia has been called a kingdom of wine. There are no other shops in Volpaia.

Also at the castle is the Osterio Il Tocco. In the piazza is the restaurant La Bottega and Caffè Bar-Ucci – a central stage for the following story. The Barucci family, mother Gina, father Oriano, and daughters Carla and Paola are central figures in this narrative.

# WEEK ONE

## Sunday, domenica, September 20, 2009

"*I* write for myself. It is important to me that my audience is me…not others. The thing is in the writing – this moment! That is, I want to focus on my experience rather than on how this will appear if read by others." This is how I began this diary. Soon, however, I became quite conscious of potential readers and of my desire to have you, the reader, join us in your imagination.

Our journey from Seattle included a day in Paris where we enjoyed a lunch at a café with an Italian couple (from near Venice) seated near us. She started singing O Sole Mio and then Nessun Dorma (a signature song of Pavarotti). I joined her. The couple understood my broken Italian! I realized that my year at La Scuola Italiana in Seattle had prepared me to better speak and hear this enchanting language.

Upon our arrival last night in Volpaia, Paola, Gina, and Carla greeted us as if we were family - like when our children and grandchildren were young and would open their arms and raise their voices and run to us.

Patricia described it in her dream chronicle where she makes occasional notations about daily happenings; "Arriving in Volpaia! The look on Paola's face as she shouted, 'Professore!'. She and Roberto greet each other like long-lost siblings. Hugs! Kisses – and then Carla runs across the piazza to embrace me and then Roberto – everyone at the top of their voices including Mamma Gina!"

That marvelous spontaneity is alive in them! That is one reason why I find them so easy to love!

My first day here and Mass is at ten in the towering centuries-old stone church in Volpaia's piazza. At Mass I sat in front of Gina Barucci, the matriarch of the family. She sings well and heartily. I was surprised at the pronunciation of Amen. It sometimes sounded like "Aum" or "Awom" in nearly one syllable.

I have high respect for Hinduism and its ancient scriptures. That sacred word A-U-M (or Om), is considered not only to be the original sound of creation, but the Supreme Brahman itself. "Itself" is accurate. The god Brahman (Brahma) – It does not exist – It is existence – constantly expanding! The goal is to experience one's self as being one with existence – one with Brahman, that is, "to make (have) your heartbeat match the beat of the universe.)[4] I experienced this moment as universal which is the meaning of the word "catholic". Today I am catholic in the spirit and culture of this community and celebrating the essential oneness of all. The priest knows that I am not a Roman Catholic. I told him last year when he invited me to sing at Mass. His response: "It doesn't matter".

Afterward at Caffè Bar-Ucci, Paola stood beside me and started our ritual where she begins and I sing the next phrase of "O Sole Mio".

Paola Barucci of Caffè Bar-Ucci has become a soul mate over the years. Most of our children are older than her, but we are holding Paola, sister Carla and their parents – Gina and Oriano – as our "family" – a special connection. And – oh yes – Pallina, part Labrador and Ombra, a spaniel.

Frequently we sing improvised tunes to go with whatever we are "saying" but mostly we sing music such as Nessun Dorma, Una Furtiva Lagrima, Che Gelida Manina, Santa Lucia or Brindisi, Verdi's toast from La Traviata. Other arias and Italian folk favorites grace the air, usually accompanied by a glass of wine.

Joyous, raucous, Bacchus – the Roman god of wine and festivity!

Soon the rains came – those marvelous thunder and lightning storms which carry the primal energy of ancient gods that refresh and renew the very air surrounding us. Oriano and I sat here and talked as the rain subsided. He speaks no English. Limited as our conversation is now, a year ago it was impossible. Oriano is 79 years. He spoke of the Second World War as "brutal". He was fifteen when the war ended and I was seventeen in my protected environment across the Atlantic. We agreed to talk more later.

Medieval Volpaia is enchanting, but of course, it's really our friends who draw us here. Already my expectations are exceeded.

Soon, at Caffè Bar-Ucci, I was singing for Brazilians again – 15 months after our first encounter with the same tour guide who invited me to repeat the previous performance. This time I started "O Sole Mio" which puts Paola, in her turn, to sing the high note at the end, but she always catches on and switches the ending back to me. It's a fun game

---

4. Joseph Campbell Companion, Diane Osbon, Harper-Collins, ©1991, The Joseph Campbell Foundation.

we play. Then we went to our "home" in Volpaia. To celebrate, I bought a bottle of Pruneto wine made only a short distance away. I met the winemaker, Ric-cardo Lanza, at Caffè Bar-Ucci years ago and often rested on a stone by the winery's hand-painted sign while walking up the one-lane "Roman" road with it's ancient lichen-ladened stone walls. I then continued on my way to the refreshing fountain in the piazza years before we moved here.

## Monday, lunedi (Moon), September 21, 2009

*I* like that, in Italian, the days of the week are named for planets. It is easier to remember.

Caffè Bar-Ucci is closed on Mondays. I'm sitting on the bench in the piazza from which Oriano and Gina often watch life go by and engage with friends such as Lina who is seated to the right in the photo and Pallina, their lab.

The piazza. Everything emanates from this square in the center of the village. It is the heart of the heart. All paths lead to and from here. Excitement is engendered. Grief is shared. Celebrations emerge. From this center, one goes home at night and returns in the newness of the morning. It is as if life begins in the piazza again and then again.

Witnessing life from the bench as it unfolds each day, one may see people entering the weathered sandstone church. Today some are reading the menu at the entrance of La Bottega which has a garden restaurant, shaded by a floral canopy of red and green, and a soft cream eye-appealing interior setting. Chef Carla Barucci may often be seen crossing the piazza pausing to affectionately hug Pallina and Ombra, the canine members of the family, either of whom may be frolicking or sleeping where cars must maneuver to avoid crushing them. A cat may scurry rapidly across the whole width of the piazza chasing whatever it is that cats chase. Also, bikers and hikers from many nations roam by and often stop for nourishment at Caffè Bar-Ucci, La Bottega, or Osterio Il Tocco in Castello di Volpaia. The castle protected the countryside 500 years ago. Some just entered the castle's shop near the bench, searching for olive oil pressed on site, Volpaia's respected wines, or their red and white wine vinegars. The bench from which all of this unrehearsed action may be seen is cradled against the greenish-gray sandstone wall of this 13th century castle. With the light green and white Ivy geraniums cascading down above a vibrant red post box, this modern function meshes with the ancient stone wall. The bench holds memories of myriad conversations. Communication happens here!

Today few come and go. The birds sing. Pallina rests in the middle of the piazza, her black lab coat contrasting with the sand-colored surface. A car weaves around her. Gina calls, "Buon Giorno Professore!" and invites me for a "caffè". I will not resist that call.

Life seems so simple – so tranquil.

So Gina gives me a cappuccino and invites me inside La Bottega as it is chilly outside. I study my Italian and experience the busyness of the morning prep. Supporting the peacefulness and the spontaneous opportunities is the careful preparation – the order. A philosopher once wrote, "There is no freedom without structure". The grounding for spontaneity and festivity lies in careful planning and hard work by someone, somewhere. Supplies arrive, garbage goes, and outside tables are cleaned. The day has begun.

Gina and I, haltingly, conversed. I think we understood each other. I told her that I liked her singing at Mass and that I would be singing Ave Maria at the next Mass. "Schubert?" she asked. "Si!" Little did I know how much these people love Schubert's Ave Maria. I would soon learn. One more coffee and then Patricia and I take off to Radda which lies only a few miles away. From Radda one can see endless fields of vineyards and the companion olive trees with their silver manes tossing in the wind. In the distance lies Volpaia nestled near the top of the mountain.

We ate lunch at Carolyn's, our British friend, who married an Italian and began her café called Bar Dante Alighieri where Via Roma meets highway S.R.429. It is a quaint example of the art of dining al fresco in Italy. We are served pappardelle con (with) cinghiale (wild boar). She also features exquisite wines of the area served by the glass. Around the corner there are sycamore trees like those from my boyhood life in Pennsylvania in the USA. It is one world.

## Late Afternoon

*I* am sitting alone at my favorite table on the tent-covered porch of the empty Caffè Bar-Ucci. At my back is an ivy-covered lattice. To my right is the back of the fountain which cooled me for years when, from our rental villa about a mile away, I daily walked up the ancient narrow unpaved road to Volpaia past isolated dwellings, terraced vineyards, olive orchards, stone walls, and finally through a cathedral of cypress trees, a sacred grove for me. I arrived in the piazza thirsty and perspiring. At my first sight of the piazza, Caffè Bar-Ucci loomed large and the fountain appeared as an oasis for this tired old hiker.

So "my" table is steeped with memories. And from it now, I can see the happenings in the piazza as well as at Bar-Ucci. I love the privacy of

having my own defined space, though it is claimed at times by unknowing others who arrive before I do. I dream here. I create! I sing! And today I penned the following:

> In the piazza again greenery abounds
> midst shades of red
>
> The dog chorus was in preparation
> for the concert later [5]
>
> But now there is only the wind with occasional voices
> drifting-by.
>
> The beginning of fall is in the air.
> How I love this place!
>
> What creates this space, any space,
> as paradise?

As I ponder; Paola greets me and walks up the stairs to her home. I continue writing.

So today Bar-Ucci is closed, but not for this moment. I look up from my writing and a glass of wine has appeared before me on the table. No one is here but me. Paola came and went. Like life!

I would not learn until a month later that my beloved friend Giulio di Furia had left us. He had taught me Italian pronunciations of arias seated in the hot tub in our condo in Seattle. I was in his beloved Italy, while this gentle man was being mourned in Seattle.

So I ask about paradise and a moment like this happens. The death of a dear friend, though out of my awareness in this moment. Here and now, a friend comes and leaves. "I always walk

---

5. Late each evening, the canine chorus begins. From the distant northeast hill, first one soprano and then dozens of others begin the nightly concert. Soon, from the hills to our west, a lone bass is joined by many others who, I'm sure eagerly wait each evening to serenade us in the valley – at least those of us who have stayed awake long enough to be enchanted by this acappella barking choir. And then, from the southeast comes one tenor and many other tenors, singing their version of Donizetti, Puccini, Rossini, and ah, yes, now I hear one of those engaging Verdi choruses. It is one more time of magic, gifted to Patricia and me as we sit by our mulberry tree under a brilliant starlit sky. (written in 2004 when we lived in La Capanna, a mile from Volpaia, owned by Enrico and Rita Tanzini)

right next to death, just a touch away", I wrote in my middle years when especially impacted by the death of my older brother. "This presence need not morbid be, nor need it be denied. I simply brush reality to know it's at my side".[6] A brief engagement. A spark of existence. La dolce vita – the sweet life. I'm suddenly aware of a bee in my beard as I write this. Is it to be feared or to be seen as a vision of a taste of honey? Or both? So I "brush reality". The older I get the more I "brush" the immediate passing moments of life with alternating joy and sorrow.

With my stumbling Italian language knowledge, I spent the next two hours, dictionary at hand, translating the above verse about the piazza for Paola. I hope it was close enough!

It is evening at the Osteria Il Tocco in the castle. We joined some Canadians. One of them was celebrating both her birthday and her engagement that day. We sang lustily, especially Verdi's Brindisi from La Traviata which all sang (la, la) regardless of whether each knew the words. It's about spirit. Words are secondary.

Despite what I have just written, I acknowledge that the words to Brindisi are especially relevant to such a festive occasion. Brindisi means "a toast". This one is to love, sweetness, and warm kisses ending with an admonition to "discover this day"! The tune is easy to sing and any occasion is made even more joyful and robust when this chorus is raised.

<hr>

6.  Complete poem in appendix A.

## Tuesday, martedì (Mars) September 22

*T*oday is a simple day for me. I'm at Bar-Ucci for several hours before Patricia joins me for a classic lunch of ribollita, the Tuscan special soup made by Gina , and crostini neri (a liver pate) which both we and a village black cat find delectable.

While Patricia lingered at Bar-Ucci, I crossed the piazza with Paola, at her request, to sing Ave Maria in the church. Patricia soon began to hear my voice from her seat at Bar-Ucci. In editing my diary she noticed that I made no mention of this moment. "I don't know how to write about it." "Then I will," said she. Here is her story.

"Echoing, reverberating from the ageless stones that formed the soaring walls and domed ceiling of the church, the strains of Ave Maria seemed to be from a disembodied, almost unearthly voice across the piazza. The crowded café grew quiet, each person apparently struck by the other- worldliness of it all: the medieval village, the ancient church, that hymn. Perhaps for some, at that moment, they realized their own quest which had brought them here  on that day. The applause and appreciation carried across the piazza, and increased as people began to realize that the mysterious sound was not a recording, but from the person now walking from the church entrance to the café porch."

My impact surprised, delighted, and embarrassed me, especially as I later heard Patricia's story of the event. Again, I am face to face with acclaim and my inability to receive it and drink it in. It seems like a human dilemma. How often I've seen others turn their head away without acknowledging even a simple thanks. I've admired Luciano Pavarotti's style of opening his arms and smiling radiantly as he received thunderous applause. The response coming from those at Caffè Bar-Ucci exceeded my own self concept. Merton's "unaccepted self" as quoted in my introduction looms its head again and again.

After a nap we drove to Radda to shop at macelleria Alimentari Porciatti in the piazza for produce that Patricia will prepare at our villa. Interacting with the owner, Luciano Porciatti, his sister, Anna, or sons, Riccardo and Francesco, we buy favorite treats such as cipolline onions in balsamic vinegar, nutty-flavored pecorino cheese, marinated fresh anchovies, and an array of char-grilled vegetables and freshly butchered meats. A wide array of wines grace their shop. On one visit I found a favorite sauvignon,  Ronco delle Mele of the Venica & Venica Winery. It will be warm enough to dine with the food purchased here at our greenery-roofed veranda where the calico cat and the village black cat will join us.

As evening falls we returned to Bar-Ucci for Fernet Branca, a few songs with Paola, and then again, Ave Maria in the church. After I stop a phrase, the echo continues for 2-3 seconds. Unbelievable!

As is life!

Ombra ("shadow" in Italian) the dog, and the village black cat with us in the church, agreed.

## Wednesday, mercoledi (Mercury) September 23

*I*'m off, as is my daily custom, to Bar-Ucci this morning. A couple is seated here who were at Monday night's party in the Osteria. The woman has a beautiful gentle voice and she started singing "her" song for the day and then asked for mine. Together we sang "O what a beautiful morning" with me singing a line and she the next as I do with Paola! It was a warm memorable exchange with someone who I'll probably not meet again but will remember.

As they left I turned to Oriano who had just arrived and said, "Le dispiace se le chiedo della sua vita?" ("Would it displease you if I asked about your life"?) This is a phrase of courtesy I had learned from Doria Reagan in Seattle. "No, No," he responded. I learned that he and Gina had moved to Volpaia, and therefore "the shop" (La Bottega) in 1979, the year of their 25th Anniversary. After remodeling, La Bottega later moved to its beautiful interior and exterior on the other side of the church. They now live above that space. The "shop" has a 300-year history. I also learned that both of his parents died in the war that he had called "brutal". The only Italian available to me in that moment was to say, "I'm sorry". I felt it deeply as our eyes met and lingered briefly.

Carla just walked by with a warm "Buon Giorno". And Paola arrived as only Paola can arrive – very alive! I think I'll order Oriano's salumi with fennel – none better!

I just met David and Marie who are French and live 15 meters from us. He is a pianist and they invite us for an hour of singing sometime soon.

Orazio Semplici, the bread man cometh! One euro! For 56 years Orazio has baked the same bread!! In Tuscany there is no salt in the bread creating a texture of crunchy crust and soft chewy interior. Of course, it is also influenced by that unique Tuscan sun, soil, and air which have been protected for centuries by laws limiting deforestation and by strong cultural customs against chemical fertilizers. The forests

remain plentiful in Chianti. Flies are rare in Volpaia and mosquitoes even rarer. The bread is also enhanced by brick ovens and the touch of the artistic, proud breadmakers. With a hard crust, even after it is broken open it remains fresh for days. Left over, it is used in many unique Tuscan dishes such as Gina's ribollita.

Soon a group of hikers arrive with joyous voices matching Paola's. Having walked the back unpaved road from Panzano, they celebrate with coffee and wine. The language is French and Italian today. Yesterday it was German and Argentinean Spanish. Tomorrow?

Toward noon we left for the village of Panzano by that same winding unpaved back road where the deer and the cinghiale (wild boars) play. It is also where the chestnut trees thrive that a century ago were dominant in the eastern USA. Our honey of choice is that dark brown, woodsy-flavored gift from the chestnuts, the bees, and the keepers of these tiny wild ones.

Dario Cecchini, whom Wine and Food magazine has called; "the most famous butcher in Italy", was not there. His macelleria (butchershop) is closed for business on Wednesday but Kim, who will soon be his wife, was there. His shop is a dramatic event. Entering on the right, there is a table full of snacks such as meat loaf with his "mustarda Mediterranea", a sweet and spicy red sauce. Last year I had a case shipped to Seattle for my 80th birthday.

Upon returning from Panzano, we went, of course, where else but to Caffè Bar-Ucci.

I had a delightful brief encounter with Oriano who asked in Italian, "Where did you go today"? I was pleased that I understood his question. As we talked, I drank a Sambuca "con tre mosche" – which has a fun history for us from a time in Gaiole when a man tried to convince us that mosche meant "mosquitoes". Actually it means "fly" which is represented in the Sambuca by coffee beans.

Then I spoke to Lina Selvolini. Volpaia is, I'm told, a rare small village where almost everyone speaks only Italian with few learning English!! Of course, the castle employees who arrange our rentals speak English.

In a brief conversation with Lina at Bar-Ucci, I learned that her family took up residence in Volpaia 310 years ago. With my new-world roots in me that seems to be forever! Yet, my ancestors came to the east coast of the new world over 300 years ago. Why don't I feel the continuity? Is it because they came to a wilderness more than 3000 miles from where

I now live? Certainly I'm not in the same village. The people who lived in the Pacific Northwest then were untouched by Western civilization. My DNA tells me (as does my intuitive spiritual self) that I am one with them and them with me. But in my cultural upbringing, I didn't think that way. Since my birth, I've lived in fourteen towns and cities.

Years ago, in St. Emilion, France I pondered this same question when I wrote:

> "I wonder what it means to live
> Amidst a timelessness like this.
> Imagine as a little one
> To know that where I live I'll die."
> ……and then later in the poem,
> "I do not like my rootlessness,
> At least, not so today.
> I want to feel my roots run deep,
> And have the simple sense
> Of who I am, from whence I've come
> And where I'll finally rest in sleep"[7]

After twenty years in our Seattle home I have much more of a settled feeling than when I wrote that. Twenty years! Lina has her lifetime, her family's 310 years and Volpaia's thousand!

For dinner at Frantoio (our rental home) we sat in our garden dining space with its living green roof draped with long-trailing lavender wisteria buds. The slate-like stone floor emanates coolness, and the lavender color melds into the stones of the surrounding walls, soil, and roofs. Dining in a gentle cleansing rain, the sweetness of the lightly perfumed floral aroma surrounds us as drops of water slowly begin to join our earthy moment. Frantoio is an appropriate designation for this space. The olive by that name is highly prized. We ate Oriano's fennel salumi, a local pecorino cheese, avocado, grilled red peppers and fittingly, olives plus the local olive oil on Orazio's bread. We basked in the tranquility. Our bottle of house wine from a nearby vineyard cost 5 Euros.

---

7.  complete poem in Appendix B

The tranquility – what did it cost? To be present in the moment.
To accept what is – now. To be free of "what if" – to accept that I am and
we are exactly in the right place, the right space within ourselves and
with each other – now. As a hyper-active boy, I learned what became a
favorite quote, "In quietness and in confidence shall be your strength."[8]
Being in such a space was a huge and needed step for me then and that
quest continues.

Patricia noted, "Utter quiet at night – only crickets or an occasional
distant car after 8 or 9PM. Peace…peace."

In the Hebrew scriptures it is written, "…the Lord is not in the wind,
earthquake, or fire, but in a sound of sheer silence"[9] Perhaps when
allowing ourselves to find and savor such a moment, we tap into the deep
wisdom of the universe.

In the Garden of Eden. In Paradiso – The paradise of love, life, self,
other, and the community that one is in at this moment – this day.

---

8. Isaiah 30:15
9. I Kings 19:12 New Revised Standard Version

## Thursday, giovedì (Jupiter) September 24

*I*t is a quiet day for us in Volpaia. Patricia loves to cook and has enough of what she needs to begin her process without going to Luciano's in Radda or even, at Paola's invitation, picking some basil growing just outside the café.

My job in Seattle and here is to match wine with food and do the kitchen cleanup. With her wonderful unfolding cooking process pots and pans accumulate as well as dishes. But, oh my, the result which, lucky man that I am, I taste tenderly while often asking to hear the step-by-step development of what now rests on my plate.

"Marriage is … the grace of participation in another life…. Successful marriage is leading innovative lives together, being open, non-programmed. It's a free fall: how you handle each new thing as it comes along."[10]

We strolled down the narrow cobblestone street to Bar-Ucci. David dropped by to invite Patricia and me for Saturday night dinner and singing. Soon, Paola, other customers and I were singing Arrivederci Roma and then the lines from Che Gelida Manina where the poor artist asks "How do I live?" and then answers "Vivó!" (I live!). After the apertif, we basked in our outdoor dining area. In the garden next to us, a  last rose of summer blessed us every time we looked her way.

---

10.  A Joseph Campbell Companion, Diane K. Osbon, Harper-Collins, © 1991, The Joseph Campbell Foundation.

## FRIDAY, VENERDÌ (VENUS) SEPTEMBER 25

*I* awoke to a sunrise of pink ribbons floating across the mountains behind Radda. I love the morning. Wrote the Trappist Monk Thomas Merton in *Journals,* "It is necessary for me to see the first point of light that begins to be dawn. It is necessary to be present alone at the resurrection of Day in solemn silence at which the sun appears, for at this moment all the affairs of cities, of governments, of war departments, are seen to be the bickering of mice. I receive from the Eastern woods, the tall oaks, the one word DAY. It is never the same. It is always in a totally new language" (Merton, 1965, p.VII). There is a new birth every day and it is called sunrise. The pink ribbons expand and then recede as bits of fog hide behind the hills. I step outside to see a broader horizon and to breathe deeply the moist air. Too quickly for me the first colors – pink, white, blue, and tinges of gold – recede and a deeper blue fighting for dominance with the radiant sun emerges.

Walking to our car I see the woman, Nuccia Manganelli, with whom I talked last year. My feeble Italian had left us to mostly depend on gestures and a dictionary. I often thought of her in Italian class when I was asked, "Why are you learning Italian?" I told her that I remembered (as she did also) our talk and wanted to converse more this visit. Nuccia's husband Tullio and I exchange greetings often in our comings and goings. It was a brief exchange with a promise of more to come.

Back at Frantoio, Patricia later wrote, "Jet lag has stayed with me longer than I expected. Sleeping late I enjoy drifting in and out of sleep in the crisp mornings while I watch the sheer long curtains blowing in the window. It is so quiet that one can hear the breeze. This while Roberto is at Bar-Ucci making aquaintence with everyone from all over the world as they roam by. The time spent in my peaceful, still, dark room is meditative – a non demanding sanctuary."

Later we drove to the market in Radda and afterwards visited with an old friend, Miranda, at Villa Miranda, whom we know from our first year in Radda. Her roots run deep. Her family bought this land in 1800, and she was born in the room above the restaurant. She remembers, with deep emotion, that at age five the Americans came through Radda and gave her chocolate. She has, ever since, loved America and followed our evolving history. Our current direction has her even more excited about the U.S.

Her food is exquisite – pappardelle con cinghiale for Patricia, ravioli con tartufo (with truffle) for me. The outside dining garden, contrasted to her interior dining, is not tidy enough for many. We see tourists take one look and go inside. The canopy of towering trees surrounded by vines, and the constant dropping of seeds and leaves in the fall, would make it difficult to perfectly care for this rustic space. We love it and have a favorite corner table.

The excellence is in her food. She's up before 5 AM to prepare the bread and fresh pasta for the day. Then she chooses the herbs and tomatoes to create the sauces in which she'll use her own olive oil and wine made by her daughter. Her bruschetta, liberally moistened with her fresh olive oil, ranks with the best. In Chianti, the cuisine contains the essence of the land. There is a profound, sacred kinship between the various food elements, the wine, the sun, and those who nurture, plant, and harvest. In the kitchen these are melded by a deft hand into a harmonious sensual delight.

We talked for at least an hour. Miranda speaks only Italian. Before, with Miranda, we could exchange greetings but nothing else. Now we talk of family, history, the war, and current politics!

Back at Bar-Ucci we hear, from the piazza bench near "my" table at the café, Nuccia's resonant voice, Gina's rapid fire speech, Oriano's frequent, but brief interjections and finally Paola walking down her steps (she lives above the café) and her entry to the porch of Bar-Ucci. Then arrives Nancy from Iowa who is renting from Lina. I just translated for her with Lina! Me, the translator!! How much did I mistranslate?

Thank you Tina Morelli of La Scuola Italiana. Oh yes, yesterday we saw a bus labeled "scuolabus". Why not one also, Tina, in Seattle to pick up your students!

## SATURDAY, SABATO (SABBATH) SEPTEMBER 26

*I*n Radda yesterday at Paolo's Caparsa Wine Shop on Via
Roma, we arrived at the very moment as two Dutchmen
who were searching for the wine shop that sold a previous book of mine.
They had seen the picture of Caffè Bar-Ucci in the book yesterday in Volpaia. From Paola they had learned to call me Professore. Upon leaving the
shop I left my sun-glasses and newspaper. One of the men shouted with
glee, "Now we know for sure that you are Professore!" They were referring
to the absent-minded professor stereotype.

Then we are off to see Paolo at his Caparsa Winery and Vineyards.
We forgot our groceries and had to return later proving that both Patricia
and I had indeed been professors. Actually, in technical usage, we had
been faculty and instructors not with the designation "professor". But,
long ago, let it be known across the land, I was so anointed by Paola
Barucci herself, the highest authority for such matters! It is like at Pike
Place Market, in Seattle, where, 20 years ago, I was anointed "tenor man"
by those harmonious African American brothers of mine with whom I
have often been privileged to sing and by my singing companion of 20
years, the late Jim Hinde.

Paolo has been our friend now for ten years. What a magnificent time
with Gianna and their entire family coming and going. Federico is now

tall, handsome at 20 years. I remember him at 10. The next son Felippo is 16. The only daughter Fiamma is 7 and the twins Francesco and Flavio are 4. It was delightful to see children playing with horse chestnuts rather than plastic toys. They live in this gorgeous environment with a father who

values organic farming, and who is proud that the deer and rabbits feast on his grapes where pesticides are never used.

I have written about his pride in being known as, "a peasant, not just an owner." This time we learned much more about his roots and our compatibility. His father was an activist and an author supporting "peasant" causes and equality among people. Father can be proud of his son! Paolo gave me a copy of his father's book, "Veglie a Porcigrano" by Reginaldo Cianferoni.

He is reading the Italian translation of my "Authentic Leader" which reflects that same concern for "peasant". I dedicated that book to my father, the working man and steelworker union member. Paolo gifted us with his smooth non-filtered olive oil with its delightful peppery finish. He also gave us his Doccio e Matteo, year 2000, which received the highest possible rating in the Italian wine book Gambero Rosso – Three Glasses. His Caparsino Chianti Classico wine is also a special favorite of

ours. Paolo's wines have a delightful earthiness. Non-filtered and aged in oak barrels for 18 months, they are elegant whether opened young or after years in the bottle.

I took a picture of the Doccio e Matteo vineyard at the crest of the hill to show to my grandson Matteo.

Later we return to Volpaia and I sit at my oasis, Caffè Bar-Ucci. The activity today as I sit at my table is similar to other days with different visiting tourists but the same main actors, actresses, cats and dogs.

Across the piazza (75 feet) I shout "Buon giorno" to Gina the matriarch and she shouts back that greeting and the familiar "Come va?", not "Come stai?" as it says in my simple Italian phrase book. They both mean, essentially, the same thing. I'm told that Volpaia has a unique dialect and that Italians enjoy hearing Paola and Gina going "full speed!" Of course, we all have a "unique" dialect. We simply don't recognize our own. Only as an adult, when I saw a book titled "Pittsburgh English" did I realize my unusual use of my language! Elizabeth, one of our daughters, loves to tease me about my pronunciation of my native baseball team as the Pittsburgh "Parrots" as opposed to the Pittsburgh "Pirates".

That evening at David and Marie Sauzin's invitation we had dinner in their small corner of the castle. Dominique Garett, also French, joined us. They rented a home here a year ago and still return to Paris for one week every two months. By chance they served Paolo's 1998 Chianti Classico Reserva not knowing of our relationship with him. Also, Caspar, an Egyptian viognier and a chardonnay from the Sahara; both delightful and new to us..

With these interesting and aware people we discussed history, wine, classical music, and the DNA story of our origin learned through the National Geographic DNA testing program, it's genographic project. The story is that all humans migrated from central Africa 55,000 years ago. It is told eloquently in PBS's "Journey of Man". My story included a 20,000 year sojourn in Ethiopian territory before moving north through Egypt and the middle east. Patricia's ancestral journey was quite different. Ancestors of this classic looking Norwegian woman moved north but also to the east and west. Other lines migrated to West Africa – and later to America as slaves and to Australia (Aborigines). All share cheekbones with a striking resemblance.

After dinner, he played the piano beautifully as I sang Una Furtiva Lagrima, Ave Maria, and others, ending with Nessun Dorma. We did it three times as the accompaniment is so great and worthy of many encores. Each time my ending B natural got stronger and more assured. Grazie (thank you) Tamasa Eckert, my Italian voice teacher in Seattle! Before I began with her two years ago I could not even imagine hitting that note! I have written about living in such a way that people who are younger than you say, "It must be neat to be your age". Despite writing that, I didn't expect a stronger and higher voice at my age.

David especially liked Bach's "Benedictus" which I had also sung last year at Mass in the village church.

Yes, and at dinner we all sang Brindisi with la as the most frequent word.

Afterward, at Frantoio, just across the street from the castle, Patricia and I had our usual wonderful time together reflecting on our day – our life – our love! Grow old along with me!

# WEEK TWO

## Sunday, domenica September 27

*W*alking into Bar-Ucci, I notice a bottle of Miranda's 1997 Chianti Classico on the shelf. Having tasted and enjoyed it at Miranda's in previous visits my eyes light up and I ask Paola how much it costs. "Not for sale," was her answer. Miranda had given it to her as a gift when Bar-Ucci opened on April 5, 2002.

So the first year we came to Volpaia and found the café, it had just opened! I thought that it had been here forever. Nor was there a previous cafe, rather a horse stable in the distant past.

A crowd was seated on the porch. David Chrislip and Carol Ann Wilson from Boulder, friends of Tom Bellamy and Ann Foster who live in our condo in Seattle were seated there and recognized me from a picture they had seen. They invited us to dinner in Panzano next Friday at Dario's.

I met up with Patricia again. Walking through a shaded area, with fallen leaves that Patricia loves to kick like a young child would, we saw Nuccia. She has cooked here in Volpaia in a private home for 33 years. We had a spirited talk with her. Again I am stunned at the difference in understanding from 15 months ago. I'm sure I misunderstand some things (maybe she hasn't cooked for 33 years), but, really, facts like numbers are easy. Deeper knowing is more abstract and difficult than knowing facts while feelings reflected in tone, face and body movements are more available. The profundities of life stories are not easily captured without a better command of the language than I yet have.

Then we were off to Badia a Coltibuono (good land) for a mid-afternoon dinner. Coltibuono is a 1000 year old Monastery, begun as a Benedictine Abbey, and now is a residence of Lorenza de Medici who is famous for cookbooks embellished

with outstanding professional photography. Her husband, Piero Stuc-
chi Prinetti, renovated his family's estate and began making wine after
World War II. Although we have had the privilege of being here before,
we find the view from our garden restaurant table to still be endlessly
beautiful. Perhaps, even more so, as our eyes remain constantly surprised
at a landscape never fully remembered by memory or photographs alone.
It's climbing vines, carefully manicured hedges, geraniums, and distant
hills exemplify the typically lush Tuscan valley of many shades of green
with the silver olive trees intertwined. Her world renowned restaurant
is exquisite in its architectural beauty and in its simplification of classic
Italian cuisine. We like to
choose a wine from the very
estate where we are eating
ingredients likely grown on
nearby soil. With its wide se-
lection of Coltibuono wines
there is ample opportunity
to pair food served with wine
made here.

   Riccardo greeted us as
he has for nine years since he
began there. I was first here
in 1995 on a wine tour. Patricia and I arrived in 1999 and have been here
most every year since.

   Excited again by it all we drove home to Volpaia. After we turned
the corner beside Bar-Ucci, I got out delivering some books that Paola
had requested. Immediately she begins our special duet. Probably 50 or
more people are cheering – thinking, I hope, that they are hearing two
Italians singing.

   Walking towards me, through the crowd, are two enthusiastic
persons. At first I don't recognize them. Then, "It's Rita and Enrico!" They
had rented their most beautiful La Capanna to us several times and they
always treated us most graciously. It was from there that I had walked up
the back "Roman" road for years before we settled in Volpaia. On two
occasions they took us to Montacino for the Gregorian Chant Mass at the
Abbazia Sant Antimo abbey south of Siena. We greeted each other and
hugged. Their smiles were broad and contagious. I remember him making
a lavender sachet for us years ago as we watched! We still have it at home.

The red geraniums that are everywhere in Chianti graced La Capanna abundantly. In the distance one could see Volpaia.

On previous visits, Rita was always a gracious hostess who also translated constantly for us. This time I could speak, haltingly, but still directly, to Enrico. Rita, 3 years ago, edited the Italian in the book I previously wrote at Bar-Ucci. The 3rd edition now reflects her work. Giulio di Furia, my dear friend, had edited the Italian for me but I had afterwards added some Italian lyrics, that in my hubris, I was "sure" were accurate! Those additions were rescued by Rita. We left with an invitation for dinner the following week.

### LUNEDI, SEPTEMBER 28

*O*ff to Gaiole for lunch. Ten years ago we began in Chianti by staying at Castello Spaltenna in Gaiole. The interior courtyard lends itself to gracious outdoor dining. With a bell tower and the church of Santa Maria di Spaltenna, it has defended and graced the area since the 12<sup>th</sup> century. In the center of town, we ate at Lo Sfizio di Bianchi, a familiar spot in the piazza. Today the lasagne was as special as we remembered. The rich glass of Querciabella enhanced it.

We discussed the difference between these delightful cities of several thousand; Radda, Panzano, Gaiole, Castellina, and tiny Volpaia. In larger towns and cities one has a circle of friends. In Volpaia the circle seems to embrace the whole place. Perhaps half the residents interact daily.

We have Volpaia fever which is a version of Tuscan fever. I do believe that one could catch such a fever in many places on the planet if one chooses to be a temporary citizen.

Previously, David and Carol had invited us to La Bottega at 7. It is David's birthday. We crossed the piazza to join them and their friends, Jay and John. In the midst of a delightful conversation the lights dimmed and Carla brought the most delicious chocolate torte imaginable with the highest possible quotient of chocolate and cream. There is one candle with Carla singing to the tune of Happy Birthday "Tanti auguri a te" (Best wishes to you) and, of course, others of us joined in the singing.

After the candle blowing out ceremony, Carla surprised me by putting her arm around me and beginning O Sole Mio – something she had never done before although Paola and I had sung it a hundred times. I treasure that continually developing relationship with her and with the others at the table.

La Bottega's outdoor dining provides an amazing vista of the distant forested hills, a nearby stately strand of cypresses and olive groves near and far in shades of silvery grey and green. The outdoor restaurant sits under an umbrella of maples overlooking the Barucci garden tended by all, but especially by Oriano, I'm told. All  this, plus friends and strangers who cease being strangers, nourishes us in this "paese" – a town that is too small to even be called a town. Village perhaps? Borgo?

MARTEDI SEPTEMBER 29, 2009

*T*he bookshelf in my bedroom has a Bible in Italian. I began this morning reading Genesis, Chapter One. Having read this often in English, it was easier to translate. I also read a favorite, Psalm Eight. I recalled music I had, years ago, written to these passages. I will ask Fred West, my choral director in Seattle to help me expand it. The leisurely pace of our life here encourages such moments of reflection and creativity.

Late morning and we again drove to Gaiole to fulfill Patricia's longing for the lasagne I had yesterday. Closed today! So we drove up the winding road to Il Papavero Osteria near Gaiole. It is sitting in the midst of a tiny village at the top of the hill in this quintessential Chianti setting. Only us to be served in the otherwise empty restaurant. The town seemed populated by cats this day. We recognize "Splash", our beloved black cat long since gone from this world. He doesn't seem to know us. Ravioli con tartufo and pappardelle con cinghiale, superb and enhanced with their house wine, is our feast. The tartufo (truffle) is a fungus, a delicacy often shaved onto pasta in this truffle-abundant land. We laugh about a possible book titled, "The futile search for bad food in Chianti".

At our last dinner in Seattle with friends, Donald Williamson asked, "What is Volpaia for you or what does it mean in your life?" I don't know. I am searching for the answer. It lies in some very deep place within. Perhaps it's the simplicity – the tranquility we find in ourselves in response to both the nighttime quiet and the Tuscan environs.

## MERCOLADI, WEDNESDAY, SEPTEMBER 30

*I*'m seated at Bar-Ucci in the early morning having found my way through an unusually thick fog. Pallina ("little ball" in Italian) is lying near me and all is peaceful in the piazza. Gina offers coffee, "un caffè", – that rich espresso treat. I choose a caffè doppio – a double shot. Oriano roams by with a greeting and then settles down at a table near Bar-Ucci's door with his coffee. Paola, usually buoyant, walks down her steps to the porch gingerly in that yawning state of waking. I hear Nuccia's marvelous deep voice approaching the piazza. The day has truly begun.

On this same morning at home Patricia noted, "Dawn came late due to a dark fog. Even at 8:30am, one can barely see a lighted street lantern at the corner. In the silence I hear the calico girl cat meowing at the kitchen door. I gave her herring and anchovies. She is so beautiful as she grooms herself on the landing, as our Seattle calico cat would do."

Soon at Bar-Ucci two Americans stop by. They had known about our history here and were curious about our relationship to this place – these people. If we don't watch T.V. (which we don't when here) and there are no shops, the inevitable question is, "What do you do all day?" Many tourists can say, "I've seen Volpaia, or I've seen Pisa," even if only once briefly. Patricia and I want more than that. I'm beginning to answer Donald's question, but what is that "more"?

In the evening, seated in our outdoor oasis, we heard Paola singing in the distance. We hurried to see her jauntily walking toward us down the road a moment later, still singing, emphasizing the spontaneity encouraged in this precious spot. We embraced. Laughed! And I caught a glimpse of that "more". To know this person and to have a unique history with her is, at least, part of the answer to the question.

*U*pon awakening from a dream I hummed a tune that had come to me. My own original or not, I don't know. It fits with a poem of mine. "Could be that in the scheme of life, when all is said and done – that I am you and you are me – and each is everyone!" I sang it over and over and wrote the notes – not trusting my future memory. The surge of creativity occurring even in my sleep state is both stirring and surprising! Why here? Why now?

I have a quiet late afternoon at Bar-Ucci as Patricia sleeps or reads at Frantoio. I'm studying my Italian textbook, occasionally talking with Paola, listening to Lina and Gina talking while sitting on the bench close by. Hearing their rapid-fire talk reminds me of how little I know of this language and the Volpaia dialect. There's a light rain today. All around us we see and smell the harvest. Paolo hasn't called for my help.

We enjoyed dinner with Rita and Enrico at La Bottega. Carla's richly flavored coniglio con tartufo (rabbit with truffle) for Patricia, cinghiale for me. Enrico's energy is as much as I remember from 2007 before an illness. Not renting from them anymore, I assumed that our relationship,

while most warm and friendly when we rented from them, was over. It's a question I've often pondered! How to measure the depth of a relationship when formed commercially. Yet, look at the depth with many in my business life.

I felt that deep bonding friendship with Rita and Enrico. No questions remain for me about how much we enjoy each other. I'm still sure that for some people "friendship" is a marketing

tool. But these relationships and others that I think of as I write transcend
the "profit motive". Rita and Enrico gave us the gift of renting a building
they had transformed into a place of beauty
graced by a centuries-old mulberry tree with
silver-leafed olive trees dancing on the terrace.
Do others wonder about these same issues- the
depth of friendship in the daily marketplace?

Thank you Enrico and Rita for helping me
to answer that question.

And what fun! As never before I spoke
with Enrico directly and not only through
Rita. We laughed – I even joked in Italian and
everyone laughed. The joke? The waiter asked
about wine and I said "Non bevo vino." (I
don't drink wine). Believe me –that is a joke. I
love the Italian blending of food and wine.

Then came singing with both Carla and Rita joining. Too beautiful.
No, not too beautiful. Vita. Dolce. Is it the slower pace here? The space is
certainly magical but almost any space can be recreated to be magical. It
just seems easier here! The ancient rural essence of Volpaia and Chianti,
I hope, flows through these pages. Chianti is a way of life, a way of being,
that nourishes one's soul with a depth that integrates the simple tasks of
life and sustenance. I thank all in Chianti who are striving to sustain,
enhance, and celebrate this!"

In eastern Tuscany we met such a man in Giuliano Tofanelli at
Palazzo di Luglio in Sansepolcro. He took extreem pride in the archway he
had built under which he served us figs hand-picked from the tree within
our view, just outside the dining room door. He proudly served the olive
oil harvested from the olive trees also within our sight and pressed by his
own hand. After a dusting of salt, he poured it tenderly on our Tuscan
bread–a celebration of life!

VENERDÌ, OCTOBER 2, 2009

*H*arvesting begins on Monday for Paolo. How does he decide? Others have already started. My text from him reads, "Dear Robert, on Monday I start the harvest of Sangiovese at Caparsa. Ciao Paolo." He has waited longer than some others but, of course, now with my help he will harvest quickly!

Talking with Gina at Bar-Ucci, I learned that she was harvesting yesterday and was tired but will be helping again each day. Such energy!

Just now there is a noise invasion! At least a dozen motorcycles – a dozen loud voices talking at the same time and drinking wine. Add to the sound a harvest tractor and trailer lumbering through the piazza narrowly missing the motorcycles parked where it says "No Parking". Decades ago in a noisy cabaret, I wrote, "How beautiful if any place, no matter what the sound… can be transformed… within my soul… a sanctuary found!"

Now here, tranquility must be found within myself!

However, soon I'm drawn into the festivities. The bikers offer me a glass of rosso. At their request I start the first line of "Brindisi", the drinking toast. Many join robustly, as noted before, singing "la, la" where they don't know the words. The tune is widely known.

Back home Patricia had written about, "… the small tractor pulling trailers full of freshly harvested grapes through our narrow streets. A vibrating sound breaks the quiet peacefulness as the grapes are being crushed near the castle immediately after picking to preserve the fresh flavor. The separated stems will become grappa." Wine is King today at the Volpaia winery!

In the evening Carol and David (with John and Jay) treated us to dinner at Dario's beautiful new restaurant, Solociccia, in Panzano. His two other restaurants across the street are Officina della Bistecca and Mac Dario. Dario was effusive. As dinner began he rushed into the room and came directly to us. As he greeted us, his mighty hug and Italian cheek-to-cheek kisses were stunning to me. Later, he gave Patricia a gift of his seasoned salt carefully wrapped by him. The group sang "Best wishes to you" to two young couples – one on their honeymoon and the other just

engaged. I was then
asked to sing a love
song to them. I chose
the last part of Una
Furtiva Lagrima "Cielo
– Heaven, I could die
of love – I could ask
for nothing more – but
love." When I started
"Cielo" it seemed that
Dario "appeared"

while I was still on the 1st note. Without
seeing him enter the room, he is suddenly there. It's like he was "beamed
up" from somewhere.

The quality, range, abundance, and ambience of this experience is
difficult to describe. It **is** an experience! To name the many offerings may
miss the essence of it all, but let's try: vegetables from fresco to frito, beans
both tan and white, beef served in spicy sauce and salad – plus Panzano's
crusty bread and olive oil cake. Punctuating all of this are Dario's very
own wine, Italian liqueurs and a buoyant temporary community of a
dozen or more gathered around a regal table in a stunning setting inspired
by this remarkable butcher!

SABATO, OCTOBER 3

*T*he "temporary citizen" theme in this journey was especially present for me at Caffé Bar-Ucci on this Saturday
morning. Reflecting on my family history I prepared to say in Italian an
insight of Patricia's that engaged me, which is, that I had lost my only sister
and Paola her only brother, and perhaps that was reflected in our close
relationship.

"My sister died when only two days old. Now you are my sister" I
successfully communicated in Italian to Paola. Her smile was huge and
immediately she embraced me across
the counter. Said both of us simultaneously "I am her fratello (brother)."
Rich moment. She said that yesterday
one of the motorcyclists had said to her
"You and professore are connected like
family" and today we confirmed it. I also
said that Carla, too, was a sister and that
I therefore have two! As a boy, I yearned
for a sister. I've found them!

We returned again to Panzano- this
time to a favorite garden restaurant,
Oltre il Giardino, with a grand view
of the valley. I asked our friendly host,
Paolo, if I could eat a grape from the
vines hanging on the lattice that created
a green "roof". "Si," he said. I did. I meandered around this lovely space.
When I returned, there was a cluster of very ripe red grapes with a sweet
tart flavor at my place on the table.

Afterwards, at Dario's butcher shop, we purchased my favorite red
sauce, his meatloaf, and a pork roast. In a reprieve of five years ago, Dario
turned on his CD of opera – the exact same one, I am sure. Again I sang
Che Gelida Manina with the recorded tenor and again I did not make the
high C.

We returned from Panzano on the unpaved back road which features chestnut trees that have grown for hundreds of years, multicolored flora and fauna, deer, farms with goats, sheep, massive cinta senese swine with their strip of white bristles on an otherwise black coat, and a rare sighting of wild boar, especially if one wanders down a side road.

We turned onto a one-lane road marked only with a modest sign reading "Cennatoio". After a half-mile drive, a place of beauty emerged. Gradually appearing was a bright barn-red two story building hovering over an empty parking lot and a wine shop entrance. Beyond it there was a striking stone estate which is the home of Leandro and Gabriella Alessi. Surrounding us as far as we could see are many acres of carefully kept fields dominated by the sangiovese grosso grapes, but also with cabernet sauvignon, merlot and a long swath of the red-leaved colorino grape crossing the length of one field in a wide band as if painted by a giant artist with a huge brush stroke.

The healthiest trebbiano and malvasia grapes for Vin Santo were already picked and suspended in "penzoli" (strings) in the vinsantaia where they dry slowly until the beginning of January. The clusters on the penzoli filled a huge barn room hanging like stalactites. The drying process was evidenced by the wilting appearance of the grape skins and moisture on the floor beneath them. In drying, a dense must develops. After pressing they are stored in small Tuscan oak casks for no fewer than nine to ten years!

We were especially intrigued with Leandro's Etruscan wine and its label in Etruscan letters – Y7SY4T3. His Bordeaux-styled wine, Sogno dell' Uva (50% cabernet sauvignon and 50% merlot), was stunningly delicious. In his broken English, he passionately introduced us to 10 of his wines, a tasting which was beyond belief. The labels are equally intriguing. Gabriella's artistic hand is evident in label after label. We met her briefly. Leandro is an artist of wine making, honey producing, and engagement with strangers who see the small sign and take the dirt road to this hidden prize – at least hidden to us. I would learn later that his wines are quite well known to major wine magazines and newspapers although we had difficulty finding them in local shops. We purchased several including his Vin Santo Rosso. All were exquisite.

Upon returning later to Bar-Ucci there were about 40 bikers here in our "tranquil" place. Despite the crowded space, Carla and Paola quickly seated us at the only empty table, bringing wine, cheese, and olives. There was a high volume of noise from many voices talking louder and louder. The inevitable happened. Paola's voice rose above the din as she announced my presence and we (for the first time with both Paola and Carla together) sang to the great applause of the crowd our theme song, "O Sole Mio." My "sisters" do not have trained voices. They sing lustily, definitely on tune, and capture the audiences' heart with their spirit.

To my surprise she then announced that I would sing "Ave Maria." Ave Maria? Really?! Now?!! Here? "Si" she replied. Well if Paola and now Carla insist, then what can a modest brother do? So Ave Maria, with reverence, as if I were singing at Mass – which I will on Sunday. Well, there was, after all, bread and wine present and a unique social community - bikers. Bikers stopped in this medieval village and I left that moment appreciating them in ways I had not imagined before.

# WEEK THREE

DOMENICA, OCTOBER 4, 2009

*I* awoke early. The sunrise had just begun, but was quickly shifting colors as the fog moved behind the hills as if rushing to avoid the heat of the new day. With such a sight I remember a favorite Thomas Merton quote. "Brilliant and gorgeous day, bright sun, breeze making all the leaves and high brown grass shine. Singing of the wind in the cedars. Exultant day, in which a puddle in the pig lot shines like precious silver."[11]

Once a year Mass is held at a 17th-century Church ½ kilometer away but inaccessible except by jeep and by foot. It is the church of the Madonna of the stream. "La Madonna del Fossato". Fossato means "moat". Often it was a boundary between properties in ancient times.

The priest had me begin with Ave Maria. The tones reverberated off the stone interior. The ancient world meets this modern moment. The Latin liturgy is given while a bird flies frantically around midst the loud voices of children with parents hushing them. The dog Ombra came in twice and was escorted out by Gina. The priest maintained a calm presence.

Forty years ago, the older Father Chuck Suver of the Gonzaga University campus St. Aloysius Church and young Father Pat Carroll (the charismatic student chaplain) differed about whether I should receive the host in the Mass on Sunday morning following the weekend trainings that I directed at G.U. I loved both of those men. For Suver, my not taking the host was a reminder of the painful brokenness of the church. For Carroll, my taking it represented a fundamental connection among Christians

---

11. Merton, T., A Year with Thomas Merton: Harper San Francisco, 2004 (Entry for October 10)

though not realized yet. It was for him, I think, a symbol of hope. While inclined to agree with Father Carroll, I always chose Father Suver's position. Often the three of us embraced and shed tears at that moment.

Today I reprised that 40-year journey. Having experienced the joy of reconciliation and the pain of separateness across the years since then, I tune into it now in this place, this community, this Mass. Beyond the brokenness that lies within each religion there is certainly also pain in the planetary community. We are all one but have not realized it yet. But I see it in everyone I meet.

I love the mystery of the Mass as we loved the liturgy in Moscow at the Russian Orthodox (wedding and funeral) services. Mystery at the Mosque, at the Synagogue – in life! If I'm sure that my beliefs are the only "true" beliefs, then mystery seems lost and the leap of faith into the not-knowing is rendered unnecessary! Faith in a doctrine whether religious or secular (scientism, capitalism, communism) is not faith for me. Fifty-six years ago I heard Howard Thurman, the Baptist mystic and mentor for Martin Luther King Jr. say, "I take a leap of faith. But always within me there is the rumor that I may be wrong! …and that's my growing edge!" I honor mystery. Today I experienced this in the Mass.

Ombra just walked by. I wonder if any dog attends church more often. Who can claim a more religious dog?

In the evening, we accepted the invitation of six Floridians, Al, two Jerrys, Barbara, Sherry and Susie to join them for dinner (catered by Paola and Carla) at Casaveccio – a villa in the Tuscan style. Lovely. A Banfi Brunello was the wine of the night complimenting my new "sisters" tasty lasagne and their unique Tuscan salad.

Al found a recording of Luciano Pavarotti singing Ave Maria on his iPod, but it kept skipping. I began to sing at each skip and then would pause and often, as if on cue, he would start again. One time, someone pointed at the silent phone and said "Come on Luciano," and he immediately began again.

Afterwards, back at Volpaia as the night slipped away, we had a poignant time in the outdoor space at La Bottega again with Andrei, the 21-year old Romanian whose mother, who lived nearby, had arrived. It was a brief moment with her, but long enough to congratulate her for having such a gracious son. All the patrons are inside, it being a brisk and cold fall evening. When Carla joins us for her cigarette break, it suddenly seems warmer and even more serene. These young men, who live upstairs to the west of the church, are full of fun and vitality and can be both playful and then serious.

We begin the goodnight walk across the piazza and then up the narrow street which goes past Bar-Ucci on our left with a six-foot stone wall on our right. Then comes the stately trees with fallen leaves that Patricia loves  to wade through. Soon we find ourselves walking up the steps with the vine-covered railings to this place that we temporarily call "home".

VENERDI, OCTOBER 5

*H*arvest day!

I begin at La Bottega. Carla offers me coffee as I write several pages in my diary. Then, I am off to Caparsa to join Paolo Cianferone for the grape harvest. Ap-

prehensively I turned off the main highway to Panzano, where just a few miles north of Radda lay his farm. I was worried that my presence would be more of a problem than a help. Gingerly, I walked to where I heard voices and soon saw activity. Paolo welcomed me with a pair of clippers and my very own bucket. After a quick training I began bending to cut the low hanging grapes. The sun was radiant. The leaves seemed brighter than usual, the grapes more robust.

If they only all hung straight! Untwisting and scraping off the rare defective or overly- dried grapes, l carried the bucket as it grew heavier. I began to sweat and appreciate the weightiness of this work. An occasional refreshing grape dropped into my mouth but I was soon hot, tired and aching from the bending. I sat down on the rugged terrain shaded by the vines and cut for a while until finally, after almost two hours, I said thanks and goodbye to Paolo. He asked me to sing before leaving. There were three hired workers, two other (Canadian) tourists, Paolo and Gianna working in this huge field as I sang the last lines of the aria that translates, "Heaven, I could die. I could ask for nothing more". Of course, Donizetti was not writing about harvesting grapes but, rather, love.

For him the elixir of love was about the love of a woman. For me, here/now – love of life; Paolo, Gianna, the workers, soil, vines, sun and the organic peasant pride of this lovely man. And yes, the grape, which with Paolo's care and artistry will soon be wine. Given his estimate that my harvest equaled forty liters of wine, many bottles of it will include the fruits of my labor. People will drink my harvest! In 1685, Francesco Redi wrote about Chianti, "robust wine..majestic, imperious, (that) wanders through the heart and unclamourously does away with every worry and every pain"[12]. That fits for me today!

12.   Francesco, Redi "Bacco in Toscana" Piero Martini all' insegna del Lion d'oro, Florence 1685

MARTEDÌ, OCTOBER 6

*I* woke up ambitious! I'll be off to harvest at Paolo's again today. Walking up the road to the car, my aches began to appear and increase! "Every pain" was not done away with! Thus, a change of plans. Harvest again tomorrow! – not today.

So now I'm at Bar-Ucci with French tourists –one being from Chinon where my father celebrated Armistice Day on November 11, 1918 after being nursed to health by a French family. Without that family–perhaps no me!

Soon Patricia arrives, her silver hair flowing in the wind. She greets me with a huge smile. When I see her my spirit lights up. It is always a special moment for me. She suggests that we go to the market at Radda, and then search for lunch somewhere new to us. Heading towards Castellina, several kilometers from Radda, she sees a sign to Osteria Le Carrozze. A lovely discovery. Gnocchi al pomodoro (small potato dumplings with tomatoes) with soft creamy bufalo mozzarella, in a quiet setting. The white-haired chef proudly serves us his gnocchi. His younger worker serves the salads and wine.

A Dutch couple arrived midway through our lunch and sat at the only other table on the small veranda. As I was leaving the man asked, "How long have you two been together?" I answered (Patricia had walked ahead looking for floral beauty) and then asked, "Why did you ask?" "Well, because you talk to each other!" I mentioned that something new constantly (even a lost memory recovered) emerges as we grow older. They seemed delighted. They are young - only 52 years old. More profoundly, our conversations are grounded in the always new moment, for unless one is able to live fully in the present, life is missed. Fresh feelings such as sadness, happiness, anger, and fear are either stimulated by our surroundings (both from the natural environment and from other humans and animals– certainly cats!) or between us. We keep current with our feelings toward each other and we recall past moments. Patricia's first forty and my first forty-nine years before we met yield memories that enlighten each to the other. Certainly in our thirty-two years since first meeting we have created our own shared stories. We also have memories and unique perceptions neither of us knew the other had.

About the time we first met I wrote,

> "I want a partner
> With whom I can dance…
> Who joins me in the quest of life
> Lived simply
> Who does not ask
> Of me
> Or us
> Or life
> Too much of what it cannot bring."

I've found that partner. As we grow older together, life brings more than I could have imagined possible. I remember, as a young man in my early twenties being enchanted by the verse, "Grow old along with me- the best is yet to be." I feel fortunate to be able to say to that poet, "How true! How very true".

Paola's forty-sixth birthday celebration really began that morning when Daniele arrived with a dozen roses for her as the day began at the cafe, and Patricia gave her a silver heart necklace she found in a jewelry store in Radda.

What a lively occasion. Twenty-six adults, one child, two dogs and a cat. Vita! Wicker-covered bottles of the Sangiovese house wine, Tuscan chardonnay, Chianti Classico, and a feast prepared by these Barucci women. Tanti auguri a te (Best wishes to you) was sung with the group, and then I added as an ending, "Tanti auguri sorella – sister". To my continued surprise the most requested song of this trip is Ave Maria. Both Carla and Paola wanted it at the party. And as always with this song, you could hear a pin drop. This beloved song touches, it seems, an even deeper chord with these people than others I've known. Whether at Sunday worship, funerals, or in the midst of a raucous Bacchus celebration, it is reverently received. Then came "Brindisi" – the toast to love and warm kisses which was among the many festive songs sung by all. It is a huge privilege to be included in such a family occasion! Since we leave before Carla's birthday on October 20th, we told her that next year we will be here for her's. We don't make such promises casually. While quickly decided by Patricia and me in an aside conversation, we mean it, the fates be willing.

GIOVEDÌ, OCTOBER 8, 2009

*O*n Wednesday, I harvested again at Paolo's. Another forty liters! I didn't even think about writing. How odd! I was more exhausted than I apparently knew or wanted to admit. I **am** eighty-one! I'm still vital in many ways but not in such a physical activity as harvesting. My appreciation has greatly increased for those, across the planet, who do such work. I bring my palms together and bow to them!

The three hired workers spoke rapid-fire Italian with Gianna and Paolo. Jokes – laughing – and rapid work. Earlier, I wrote that I will have truly learned the language when I can understand the banter in the field – or between Gina, Lina, Doina, Paola, Daniele and others here in the café. However, even with my current comprehension, I am pleased. I seem more aware, less foreign, nearly Italian! I belong more. I am weaving into the fabric of this culture.

Later back at Bar-Ucci, an American group is talking about golf and real estate in the U.S. So here/now in Paradise where beauty abounds some sit talking about commercial and sports experiences in another country. I am sure it's not only Americans who do this! Ah, some at the next table mention that they are waiting for the breadman so that they may buy a loaf of his warm freshly-made bread. Yes, may they experience this place – this moment. Perhaps I'm too critical. There must be a balance. To always talk in the here and now is too intense! But if never, then there is no present life – no intimacy.

At the next table, there are two men speaking simultaneously on cell phones in Italian and very fast so that I am not caught up in understanding. Italian sounds so melodic to me. For years, before they introduced the English sub-titles in some performances, I heard the sonorous music and words of operas without translation or a desire for it. Later I got used to the English sub-titles but sometimes found myself reading and thinking too much and missing the melodic beauty, the deeper mystery of the moment.

Once translated, soap opera sometimes comes to mind interspersed with poetic arias of the highest order. More profoundly, opera is grounded in those familiar archetypal themes that cross all cultures and time. It's just that sometimes I love to hear those rapturous sounds and not know the meaning of the words.

Off we go to Radda to the fruit and vegetable market and to Carolyn's Bar Dante for lunch. Lasagne for me and pappardelle con cinghiale for Patricia. As usual, delicious! Then home for a leisurely afternoon at Frantoio.

Patricia is not feeling her best and so has decided to stay home tonight. I'm off to Panzano and Dario's tonight with 3 Italian women!! Carla is driving. I am seated in the other front seat – Paola is in the back. Lots of jokes especially when Carla turns towards Radda instead of Panzano. "Carla, questa è la via per Panzano?" "Carla, is this the way to Panzano?" From then on I gave her directions in my suspect Italian. After we picked up Gioia (who had brought us a bottle of her homemade wine earlier) and, headed to Panzano approaching the Volpaia turn, I directed her again.

"Carla, sempre dritto!" (straight ahead). It's hard to capture the cross-language humor and laughter in those simple moments when I'm pretending that I know more than Carla about these roads that she has traversed all of her adult life!

As we approached Dario's, he was in the narrow street with his shop on one side and his elegant new restaurant a few steps across. He had stacked small glasses about fifteen high and was pouring wine into the top glass and offering it to anyone near. Kim was helping serve his meatloaf and spicy, sweet red sauce to all guests. This most festive butcher shop had instantly become the center of community and celebration for one and all.

Soon, the threads of this most amazing trip began to weave together again: companionship, food, wine, and singing.

French, Koreans, Americans and Italians – a most compatible or "simpatico" group, to quote Paola- engaged in the midst of this remarkable multicourse dinner, The wine flowed. The Korean man had brought a large bottle of "Luce", a superb Tuscan wine, of which he kindly offered me a glass.

At the other end of our table was a well-known chef from Florence's La Massa Ristorante. People periodically traded seats and the chef, Andrea, soon moved nearby. Later Carla, Gioia, Paola, Andrea and I were moving to sit and talk with others. I connected with a man on the opposite end of the table who had earlier requested Nessun Dorma which I had sung, again inviting others to join with the sounds "la, la" if they didn't know the words in Italian.

Then we sang quietly with each other – he the melody and I the harmony of "Country Roads" and a folk song favorite of his which was new to me. Later he started singing "Summertime" and many joined in as had become the custom that evening. He had a fine tenor voice and said he used to sing. What happened I asked? "Well," said he, "I'm 65 years." Hardly acceptable for this 81 year old.

Earlier when Dario started singing Brindisi, everyone had joined the festive song. In 1994 on New Year's Eve in Portland, Patricia and I had danced at a dinner concert occasion and sang with the audience when Luciano Pavarotti invited all to sing "la, la, la" as our words. Three years later while consulting at the Fusina Alcoa plant near Venice, the hourly steelworkers singing opera they loved never paused if they didn't know the words. They simply sang "la, la, la."

Coming home, all four of us joined in discussing African American spirituals and Gershwin's "Porgy and Bess" with its great song "Summertime."

At home, Patricia reflected on her quiet evening, "I'm relieved to not go to dinner in Panzano tonight. The endless struggle with language when at dinner with many non-English speaking people is exhausting for me, but exhilarates Roberto. He has put his heart into learning Italian. An important strength in our relationship is the capacity to enjoy ourselves both alone and together as life's situations arise."

VENERDÌ, FRIDAY, OCTOBER 9


*I*'ve mentioned that the most frequent question from Americans when they hear that we stay in Volpaia for several weeks is, "What do you do?" One added, "There are no stores!" I flash again on Rodolfo singing to Mimi in La Boheme, "Chi son? Sono poeta." (Who am I? I'm a poet.) "Che cosa faccio? Scrivo." (What do I do? I write.) "E Come Vivo? Vivo!!!" (How do I live? I live!!)

In the midst of this memory I look up and see that the bread man has made his daily arrival. Carla playfully tilts his hat as they engage in lively discourse! Andrei carries the loaves to La Bottega. Again when the conversation is between Italians I understand little. When between me and one or two they obviously slow down and simplify their Italian. I buy my loaf of bread from Orazio midst all of the drama around his arrival.

Life happens!

With this Barucci family, little in the present is missed. In their restaurant brochure it is written, "Living simple moments in full consciousness means to render them unforgettable in future memories." Even Ombra and Pallina, not wanting to miss the moment, crept into the picture that Daniele just took of Carla, Paola and me.

We lunched today in Castellina at Antico Trattoria "La Torre," familiar to us from our ten years in Chianti. My pizza was perfect –tomatoes, olive oil, garlic, oregano with a perfect thin crust and no cheese.

While in Castellina, we missed going to Castello di Fonterutoli. Francesco Mazzei and his Fonterutoli wines were featured at a special dinner in Seattle at Il Bistro Restaurant in the Pike Place Market. He has nearly all of its wines rated Three Glasses! Seated beside him, at Il Bistro, I had received detailed and enthusiastic stories about each wine served. His Siepi (sangiovese blended with merlot) is especially stunning, boasting a dense ruby/purple color and a rich taste with a dark berry nose and hints of vanilla.

Upon returning to Volpaia at about 6 PM, I'm sitting at my table and Patricia is at home cooking. Drops begin to tap more seriously on the tent roof of the veranda. There goes Carla walking casually in the rain to her La Bottega.

Later, after dinner at our home, we returned to the piazza and Carla's La Bottega. Despite the rain, we sat outdoors under the canvas umbrellas. Soon Andrei, Daniele, and Samir, and even the other Daniele from Poland, who works at Bar-Ucci across the piazza, showed up. He bid us a "see you later". He's off to a dance in a nearby village.

Fernet Branca for Patricia and Sambuca tre mosche for me, but mine came "cinque mosche", or with 5 coffee beans. It's Andrei's way of having fun. These Romanian young men (and three women, Doina, Nella and Zoe) at Volpaia bring their eastern European spirit to this medieval village.

I told Andrei about an article in the International Herald Tribune about the Romany. As a major article it focused on the star 5'7" soccer player Jesus Navas, "…with a turbo boost of acceleration and with a shot in either foot." Rob Hughes, the author, quotes, "Los gitanos y el futbol" by J.A. Munoz (published by the Union Romani). Jesus Navas is a Gypsy (also known as Romany).

With the depth found in the New York Times (and in their International Herald Tribune) Hughes writes about the "Gypsy integration into so many facets of life: artistic, athletic, academic." He quotes Munoz, "The funny thing is that most soccer fans do not know that many of their admired idols are gypsies. Current players like Eric Cantona, Hristo Stoichkov, Gheorghe Hagi and in the 50s the legendary Telmo Zarraonandia, or Zarro, who scored 20 goals in 20 games for Spain." I especially like this Hughes paragraph, "To say they are different, non-conformist perhaps, might be a virtue. Why should a player with touches of fantasy not light up a team the way the famed Romany dance the flamenco, play the guitar, paint or write poetry?" Such writing, such empathy, such spiritually.

After returning home from La Bottega the rains begin in a serious way. In order to enjoy the downpour we find our way back to Caffè Bar-Ucci – closed and dark; for an hour or so we sit under the tent roof on the porch, just the two of us.

Alone, together, with intense thunder and pouring rain, Patricia counts to determine how far away the lightening is from us. The display covers the whole eastern sky – a connective moment for both of us to the past – she to the lake with her father, and the memories of sitting in the rain with her beloved cat Winky. She loves a storm, as do I, but she more so. My outdoor past reaches back to 1952 dwelling in a covered wagon (a la old west) for a month which leaked when the rain was heavy. There I learned to live in the elements and to build fires during a storm using only natural ingredients such as oil of sassafras twigs found in the rain-soaked forest. For 20 years I worked nearly full-time in outdoor education.

Yes, we are present in the rain with that thread connecting us to past experiences, yet we help each other focus, mostly in the moment. She especially helps me. I preach being in the present, but easily wax philosophical, which I enjoy. She often does too – after all, she is a serious sociologist and brings a rich balance of intellect and emotional intelligence to our relationship.

What do we do all day? Live in the sunshine and the rain…in this twilight of our lives.

Patricia later mused about the romance of it all.

SABATO, OCTOBER 10

*I* woke up to a rapidly changing sunrise with a song on my lips. In the eastern sky there was a cloud and fog dance which, only moments later, condensed into small fog pockets, brightly reflecting the early sun, and then quickly dispersing as if pouring its liquid over that hill and then another. These were rapid visual shifts of light and density.

The song? Pete Seeger's "What did you learn in school today dear little boy of mine" except with the words "What did you do in Volpaia today?"

Doing or being? Much of life is framed by doing. What are you doing today? Aren't they deeply intertwined?

It seems that for us – here – a moment appears and we seize it.

All is quiet now except for the birds with their rising and falling songs! Captured by the calm, I drift toward the café and see Pallina reclining in the middle of the piazza. She rises slowly, walks onto the porch and finally settles down near the entrance. Patricia joins me in the late morning. Suddenly our eyes capture Gina walking across the piazza with a lush, newly picked green head of "bibb" lettuce about two feet in diameter.

After buying the day's bread from Orazio we cross the piazza for lunch at La Bottega. Only minutes after seeing the fabulous bibb lettuce, it became the base for fresh and crisp insalata mista. The cycle of life seems forever apparent!

In the evening we attended a concert at Castello d'Albola which had also been held in Volpaia on a previous evening. Paola had alerted us at that time by rushing to Frantoio and shouting from the street that we must come quickly to the church. Seven music historians were singing from an original, large, aging, brown, 17th-century manuscript which most had not seen before. This sight reading was from music derived from

Gregorian chanting. We were the only attendees in the ancient chapel with its sonorous acoustics. The occasion was funded by Castello d'Albola and Castello di Volpaia. These two castles along with Castello di Brolio have

a long history together. From the castle tower in d' Albola during the Siena vs. Florence wars, flares would signal those in Castello di Brolio and Castello di Volpaia of impending attacks.

Upon our arrival at Castello d' Albola we found the scholars in the wine tasting room and joined them for an aperitif. The whole group was then guided through stone passageways and a garden with fresh flowers and vegetables and then a long row of cypresses within the castle grounds to the Chapel. The journey included a stop in a wine storage area with barrels, each holding what will be 4500 bottles of wine. In another dimly lit room there were bottles from the 1950s totally covered with a natural mold substance that, we're told, helps protect the quality of the wine. A 1956 bottle had recently been opened and tasted well. How I wish I could have tasted it! We were the only audience present. The concert consisted of singing amidst pauses to discuss the documents. The small stone structure, many centuries old, resonated with a cappella sounds.

Afterward, we watched the sunset over Volpaia from Castello d'Albola. The sky was a sharp bright red with orange and silver-capped by a dark cloud suspended over Volpaia several kilometers away. "Red at night – shepherd's delight" said our Italian host. Shepherds there, but in my growing up it was "sailor's delight".

What did we do in Volpaia today? Well, we followed an invitation made in Volpaia two nights ago to a sister castle. We ended the evening back at Bar-Ucci with Paola and two English speaking Germans – one whistling songs from "West Side Story".

# WEEK FOUR

DOMENICA, OCTOBER 11

*G*ina just gave me an Italian lesson as I attempt to order a riccilarello, a favorite cookie. Then arrived "Un cappuccino e un riccilarello" and another lesson delivered clearly, firmly, and with motherly affection. I thanked her and then complimented her on her voice and mentioned that I noticed her singing with us yesterday as we sang "O Sole Mio!" It was her first time to join that performance! Mamma Mia! I hear it so often. Mamma Mia! Now again from Gina. And ciao (chow), what a blessed word! It is hello, goodbye, or if stuck for what to say, a way to communicate warmth and friendliness to others. The black and white cat just ran through the piazza chased by one of the dogs. A busload of elderly tourists has unloaded and they walk past. Pallina now rests near me. A village dog roams by. Gabriele calls out a spirited "Buon giorno" as he heads to the wine shop in the castle for his daily work. The day in Volpaia has commenced!

"Where are you staying?" Some have asked. My true heart answer would be "nowhere". This struggle about renting a lovely and even less expensive place or, again, Frantoio next year has sharply focused the difference between "staying" and "living". In reference to Frantoio either Patricia or I will often say "Let's go home" or "I'm going home" or "Let's eat at home tonight".

Living sometimes in Venice in 1997 and 1998 in the same rented apartment we would say, "home". Next week in the hotel in Venice before our return to Seattle, I'm sure we will say "room" i.e. "Let's go back to the room."

We come to Volpaia to live as temporary citizens in the village. We want to have a place we unconsciously call "home". Can any other place, no matter how lovely, be that for us or is it more like a place to "stay" – albeit delightful. Every place we've seen here in the village could be "home" but we now have christened Frantoio as such.

For some, living in or sleeping in and traveling throughout Tuscany, each day looking for a new place to stay, could be a fascinating goal. I honor such a travel goal but, for us, we want to experience daily life as much as one can who steps into the same stream for nearly one month each year. So for us Frantoio is "home". We come here to be "home" and a golden thread goes straight to our home in downtown Seattle. There, looking through our floor-to-ceiling glass doors and windows we see, on our small veranda, a Tuscan landscape with cypresses, red geraniums and trailing vines. A grand rosemary bush guards our condo herb garden.

As I reflect and drink my coffee, I notice Paola crossing the piazza with her hands full of celery, freshly cut from the garden. She shares her basil and some fresh tomatoes with us. Joining Gina and I, she mentions that we are leaving on Tuesday. "Tuesday?" says Gina with a trace of regret. "Yes, but next year there will be less Venice!" I say after Paola tells her we are going to Venice for a few days. "Next year more Volpaia!"

Roberta Torricelli drops by. She has helped us consider possible places to stay next year. Speaking fluent English, she worked at the castle and often helped when my grasp of Italian was questionable. For instance, at my request, she confirmed or corrected my translation of several conversations recorded in this diary.

Giacomo has just put up his jewelry display near the church entrance across the piazza. One day when it started raining he put up – alone – a huge tent covering this display to the applause and bravo's of those watching from the café. Patricia has one of his rings of Mexican amber and silver. He lives sometimes in Mexico and created this particular ring there. He is the only traveling vendor we have ever seen here.

I just translated per Paola's request, "Oh what a beautiful morning." She hummed along with me.

The village black cat came by begging. No Patricia yet, so no bites of the café's chicken liver crostini, a favorite of ours and, obviously, of the cat.

We would like to stay forever as Carla and Paola often suggest. Patricia fantasized about six months a year, but we know that life and relationships would then not be the same. "Absence makes the heart grow fonder" came not just from the pen of a brilliant writer but from the deep well of human experience.

Parting, separating, returning, and joining, winter and spring, death and resurrection – the cycle! The cycle of loss and gain, tears of sadness and then of joy, then of sadness, then…. I remember reading the eternal passage from Ecclesiastes Chapter 3 to our granddaughter Sarah.

"For everything there is a season…..and a time for every matter under heaven:

a time to be born and a time to die;

a time to plant, and a time to pluck up what is planted;

a time to weep, and a time to laugh;

a time to mourn, and a time to dance;

a time to love, and a time to hate;

a time for war, and time for peace."

She was barely a teenager then. Her response when I finished, "Gee, I didn't know they knew that much back then!" How precious! Well, they did! And often – we don't.

Showman that I am, I returned to Bar-Ucci at four at the previous invitation of a photographer, but he is not here. Paola and Daniele are rushed by a sudden crowd, so I choose to sit inside. I look at all the pictures on the wall- the handsome young Oriano and lovely Gina, little Carla and yet younger Paola. And, with sadness, I see the older brother Martino whose death at twenty-two is still mourned as I mourn my big brother, Gilmore, who cared for me. My older sister, Vida May, who died before I was born was always remembered in the emotional field of our family.

I become even more reflective and philosophical as our time here nears "winter." My DNA history places my ancestors in Italy 15,000 years ago. Much later many migrated to the north only to face harsh winters. It was a life or death issue to plant and harvest on schedule. Such a view of time was a critical issue for survival, and is still often important. In excess it gives primacy to schedule and order and squelches spontaneity. In the warmer climates with fresh fruits and vegetables available year round, "mañana" was the norm. There was more time and value for spontaneity and relationships. Certainly I find a more relaxing approach to life here in Volpaia.

I came saying I must have no expectations. But this visit has exceeded my fondest hopes, richer than ever and deeper. But if I say "exceeded" then I must have had expectations! Is it possible to have none? I think not. And worse, to paraphrase Alan Watts, expectations could lead one to miss the very experience you could be having now! In a moment of impatience, Joseph Campbell was admonished by Watts not to expect what isn't happening, but rather to enjoy the experience of what is. Campbell then wrote, "That's an example of what fear and desire do. I desired (a certain) situation to be the one planned, and that desire forbade me my immediate experience: This is it! This is life! Look at it! Isn't it bubbling?"[13]

Surprise! I look up and the photographer has, unaware to me, arrived and is taking photos. Ombra joins us and I pet her as the shooting continues. Just then Andrei arrives! I learned more about Martino from him. Life and death! Seasons! I reflect on "seasons" in relationships.

Learning to set aside tension in certain moments, but to not let it simmer forever, is an art of finding the right season. The key to relationship may be to balance individual private time with togetherness – the artful balance. The right time – the daily rhythms of life.

In the evening we enjoyed a leisurely dinner prepared by my favorite chef, Patricia, under the lush green cover of our outdoor dining room. The cats again joined us, enriching our enjoyment of food, space, wine, our furry friends, and reflections of a day well lived. The tall twin trees, viewed in the distance, waved.

13.  The Joseph Campbell Companion, David Osbon, 1991, Harper-Collins Publishers.

LUNEDÌ, OCTOBER 12

*M*y coming set off a flurry of barking as I approached La Bottega with its lush floral surroundings. Oriano was seated on the top step of the outside stairs, at the entrance of his home above the restaurant. A dog, strange to me started barking, and then Pallina joined.

On Mondays I go to La Bottega, sit down and begin writing. From the kitchen at the far end emerges Carla saying, "Buon Giorno, Professore . Cappucino?"

No breakfast is served here and I'm the only one seated in this early morning dimly-lit room. Soft cream colors are etched with gentle copper tones and an orange–red tile floor. About a dozen watercolors, framed in dark wood, grace the walls. They depict facets of Volpaia past and present.

Imagine that someone would write a bestseller about Volpaia. Would it be the end of the Volpaia I love, or the evolution into something equally or even more precious. Would there be more venders (now Giacomo is the occasional one) in the piazza? Would shops open? More people come? Would these eat away at the fabric of this medieval town? Of course. Even in the few years of our temporary life, in or near Volpaia, shifts have happened. Nothing stays the same.

Four years ago Carla proudly walked us through the then being constructed La Bottega. While it has been "The Shop" for 300 years, its evolution has been from the west side to the current (opened 1996) eastside spacious outdoor seating under mature maple trees. Earlier I wrote about this vista which matches the best Tuscan photos with stately dark green cypresses and silver olive trees close and distant. The outdoor seating is ringed with geraniums overlooking the lush family vegetable garden.

The current interior location, opening to the garden-like outdoor setting, began its' history in December 2006.

As I'm writing Carla is walking by preparing for the day, sometimes singing or whistling and answering my clumsy Italian efforts to learn about the history of this place. But she does answer so my clumsiness works! Volpaia is not the place it used to be. No place is.

"Professore – tear up your airline tickets – stay in Volpaia forever," repeats Carla as she walks by. The trash collector comes in singing. He smiles at Carla and then engages in a spirited conversation. But then, most conversations here are spirited. Zoe, Nella, Daniele, Andrei all arrive and are, in a flash, at their tasks. A coffee for another vender. "Du deedi du de dum", sings Carla as she taskfully walks by.

Later, though Bar- Ucci is closed, I sit there alone. The bread man comes for La Bottega. We shake hands. "I'll see you next September."

There's a conflict in the piazza. A tractor arrives. There are heated discussions and finally from a white Nuovo Surgela service truck a freezer is hand lifted by the young men to the tractor which with its automatic lift raises it fifteen feet to an overhanging veranda. Again the young men, from its nesting place on the balcony, carefully move it indoors. Now down the other steps comes the old freezer. Andrei slightly slips but catches himself. I had an urge to help. How unhelpful that would have been. Action is stalled. In the midst of "heated discussion" Gina arrives and delivers a stern voiced message, turns around and walks away! Immediately the work with the tractor starts – furiously.

The colors on the wall I am facing behind the drama just described, including the brown shutters and the chimney, have the varying light to dark brown hue of humans. From this angle, the weathered tile roof appears to have light brown bubbles on the stucco colored tile. The building next to it is dominantly charcoal with touches of pink, beige, and ombre with uneven walls. The church, with its six-foot high brown cross near the entrance, is again reflecting all the human skin variations. How appropriate for a church that calls itself "catholic"- "cattolico"- universal!

As the weather shifts towards wind and rain, which Patricia loves, I wonder where she is. I head home to find her. Our patterns, she the night one and me the morning, are spatially satisfying. This will be a day to embrace – one that she will love.

We have lunch again at the Osteria Il Tocco. The chef is Ciro. His cinghiale carpaccio with truffle shavings on arugula has become a favorite of ours.

After lunch we exit to a first-class storm. We take refuge in the alleyways of the fortress designed to discourage six-foot men like me, and certainly men on horses. The storm gods are challenging Bacchus. From the opening of the covered throughway we witnessed rain and mist, whirled by funnels of wind as I have never experienced before.

I am confident that Bacchus will prevail. Even with the black of the clouds and the near-gold of the lightning, I'll put my money on Bacchus. After all, storm gods have been powerful and have inspired conquering troops in mythic stories. Now today during the harvest – the "troops" are picking grapes and making vino.

Bacchus reigns!

Paola just returned soaked from a walk. Gina arrives with a yellow rubber glove on her head, her "umbrella" and leaves singing "Arrivederci Roma". The rains cease. The rain begins again. The cycle!

In the early afternoon we visited Giuliana and Enis Vergelli. He built a fire as a chill was in the air. More so than other years we could talk and understand. We bought her castagne (chestnut) honey and her multi-flowered honey. Enis' Vin Santo, made at home, has been 5 years in its mellowing. As is her custom, she offers us various treats concluding with the nutty-flavored exquisite Vin Santo. Their home, which romantically sits overlooking the valley, is surrounded by a garden only a short walk from the  piazza. It is the first home one sees arriving into Volpaia with lavender colored vines creeping up over the time-honored stone wall.

That evening dinner at La Bottega became a Bacchanalian celebration. Paola brought porcini mushrooms from the mountains, picked fresh that day! These became the featured taste in several dishes: porcini zuppa (soup), pappardelle (noodles) con porcini, and a tenderly fried quarter-inch slice of porcini fritter which was accompanied by caprese e melone.

We were treated again to the cinghiale (wild boar) and the rare, juicy florentine beefsteak which nobody can do better than Carla! The wine was Renzo Marinai, a Chianti Classico, and Poliziano – vin nobile di Montipulciano. And, of course, unsalted Tuscan bread and olive oil with that typical light peppery finish. Branca Mente, a rare treat, was the digestive.

Chef Carla joined us at our table in this night of tears and joy! And Ombra who had joined us under the table ate her share. That soft touch with her brown paw was irresistible.

Tears did flow, especially, with Paola. Patricia and I shared our history of helping humans to realize their emotions and honor their tears! I am easily prone to tears – sad or joyful wetness.

The ritual followed, this time with Carla and me singing O Sole Mio. Then came the signature request for the song of the month, Ave Maria. Just before singing we had eaten Carla's moist, deep, dark chocolate cake. My voice was crystal clear. How often I have sacrificed sweets and cheese before singing only to be frantically clearing my throat. The red wine overcame the sugar, or was it high percentage cacao, or who cares?

So, we have dinner with our two chefs – my Italian sisters!

When we walked in, Carla greeted us and complimented Patricia on her Italian green, shear silk scarf. "Beautiful". Patricia took it off and asked her to read the label – actually the note tied to the label. It read, in my laboriously translated Italian,

Carla:,
    "This scarf has traveled:
    Made in Italy
    Exported to Seattle
    Bought in Seattle at the Public Market by Patricia
    Brought to Italy for Carla.
    Best wishes to you for your birthday next week!
    Affectionately,"
    Patrizia & Roberto

MARTEDÌ, OCTOBER 13

We met Paola at the café this morning for a short goodbye. Un caffè and riccilarello for me. Caffè doppio for Patricia and acqua naturale. Our daily communion.

Last night Carla had mentioned her planned vacation next February in Thailand. Paola's shop is closed in January. "Where are you going?" "No lo so" "I don't know" she answered.

Sitting in this veranda which to me is a sacred setting, we invited her to come to Seattle! She lifted her hands as if in prayer of hope that she could come or, maybe, as if a prayer had been answered!

She and a little of Volpaia may arrive in Seattle!

In spirit, and in our daily living, that has already happened years ago!

.

# APPENDIX A

## RIGHT NEXT TO DEATH

I always walk right next to death,
Just a touch away.
It may reach o'er and take my breath
And end my mortal stay.

⁓

This presence need not morbid be
Nor need it be denied
I simply brush reality
To know it's at my side.

⁓

Each moment then may be my last,
Each smile, each word, each deed,
If this be so then I can cast
Away my pretense need

⁓

That I be this, or I be that
And I be who I'm not.
That I be who I think you'll like,
That I be who you thought.

⁓

If every moment of my life
Be this moment – no more,
Perhaps I then can choose to be
My truthful self, my core.

⁓

This death- my wise old self
My anchor in life's fray.
I always walk right next to death,
Just a touch away.

BY R. P. CROSBY

# C*A*PPENDIX B

## IN SOUTHERN FRANCE

A window in a quaint hotel,
A village in southern France,
Wooden shutter open wide
Inviting crisp cool wind inside.

My window opens toward a tower
Built long ago near vintage vine.
Cars weave on ancient cobbled streets
Of stone from Britain exchanged for wine.

Nearby is a chateau named Ausone
A Roman poet in 383
It's hard to comprehend
There ever was 383
With new world rootlessness in me.

I wonder what it means to live
Amidst a timelessness like this.

Imagine as a little one
To know that where I live I'll die.
The cemetery I walk through
Near where people laugh and cry
And carry out their daily fare
(maybe in my back yard at home
I'll put a small stone marker there.)

I wonder what it's like to live
With death's reminder close at hand,
To read the names of family past

And see a stone reserved for me.
I do not like my rootlessness,
At least, not so today
I want to feel my roots run deep,
And have within the simple sense
Of who I am, from whence I've come
And where I'll finally rest in sleep.

BY R. P. CROSBY